MACHINES ★ AT WORK

AIRPLANES

BY CYNTHIA ROBERTS

THE CHILD'S WORLD® • MANKATO, MINNESOTA

The Child's World

Published in the United States of America by The Child's World®
1980 Lookout Drive • Mankato, MN 56003-1705
800-599-READ • www.childsworld.com

PHOTO CREDITS
© David M. Budd Photography: cover, 8, 11, 12, 15, 16
© George Hall/Corbis: 20
© iStockphoto.com/Christoph Ermel: 7
© iStockphoto.com/mecaleha: 3
© iStockphoto.com/Robert Kelsey: 11
© iStockphoto.com/Sierrarat: 4

ACKNOWLEDGMENTS
The Child's World®: Mary Berendes, Publishing Director;
Katherine Stevenson, Editor

The Design Lab: Kathleen Petelinsek, Design and Page Production

LIBRARY OF CONGRESS CATALOGING-IN-PUBLICATION DATA
Roberts, Cynthia, 1960–
  Airplanes / by Cynthia Roberts.
    p. cm. — (Machines at work)
  Includes bibliographical references and index.
  ISBN 1-59296-825-2 (library bound : alk. paper)
  1. Airplanes–Juvenile literature. I. Title. II. Series.
  TL547.R5635 2007
  629.133'34–dc22   2006023275

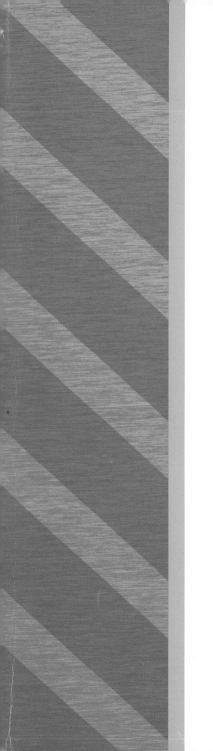

 Contents

This jet carries just a few people. Company workers use it to fly to meetings.

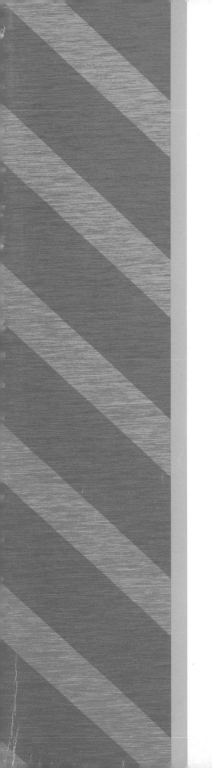

What are airplanes?

Airplanes are **vehicles** that fly. Some carry only one or two people. Others carry hundreds of people. Airplanes can go faster than cars.

What are the parts of an airplane?

Airplanes have wings. They have a tail. They have a body, called the **fuselage**. People or goods ride in the fuselage. Underneath the fuselage is the **landing gear**.

Huge jet engines like this make a lot of noise!

Airplanes are powered by **engines**. Most large airplanes have jet engines. So do some small airplanes. Other airplanes have engines with **propellers** instead. Both kinds of engines push the airplane forward.

How do airplanes fly?

As the plane moves forward, air races past the wings. The wings are a special shape. The shape makes the moving air push them upward. The plane lifts off the ground. The air holds the plane up.

air

⭐ Air flows over the top and bottom of an airplane's wings. This plane has two engines with propellers.

The cockpit is full of buttons and screens. ⭐
The pilot uses them to fly the plane.

Who flies airplanes?

In the front of the airplane is the **cockpit**. That is where the **pilot** sits. The pilot flies the plane. Sometimes other people help fly the plane, too.

How are airplanes used?

Airplanes often carry **passengers**. People use airplanes to fly all over the world. They use them to fly on vacations. They use them to travel for work. Flying is often the quickest way to travel.

Passengers sit in wide seats. There is a long walkway between them. Passengers can store coats and bags in bins above the seats.

Bags and cargo can be very heavy. Most pieces travel up a ramp into the airplane.

Many airplanes carry **cargo** instead of people. Businesses use airplanes to move packages quickly. The postal service uses airplanes to carry mail. Airplanes carry everything from toys to big machines.

Airplanes are used for other things, too. Many countries have planes in their armies and navies. Some airplanes help firefighters put out forest fires. Others dust farm fields to kill weeds or pests. Some planes are used to put on shows for people.

This airplane is spraying a farm field. The mist will kill weeds and pests.

This big jet is turning. When an airplane turns, it rolls to the side. This is called "banking."

Are airplanes important?

Airplanes are used every day, all over the world. They are used for business. They are used for fun. They carry goods from one place to another. They move things and people quickly. They are very important!

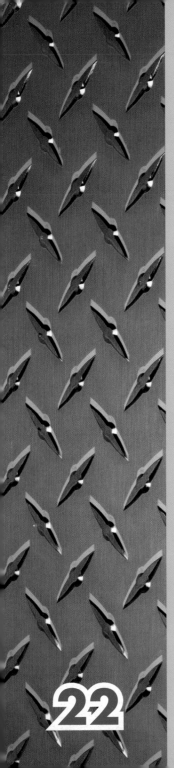

 # Glossary

cargo (KAR-goh) Cargo is gear or goods carried by a vehicle.

cockpit (KOCK-pit) The cockpit is the area of a plane or boat where the pilot sits.

engines (EN-junz) Engines are machines that make things move.

fuselage (FYOO-suh-lahzh) The body of an airplane is called its fuselage.

landing gear (LAN-ding GEER) Landing gear is machinery and wheels on which an airplane lands.

passengers (PASS-un-jurz) People who ride in something are called passengers.

pilot (PY-lut) A pilot is a person who flies an airplane or drives a ship.

propellers (pruh-PEH-lurz) Propellers are nearly flat blades that spin quickly to move a vehicle.

vehicles (VEE-ih-kullz) Vehicles are things for carrying people or goods.

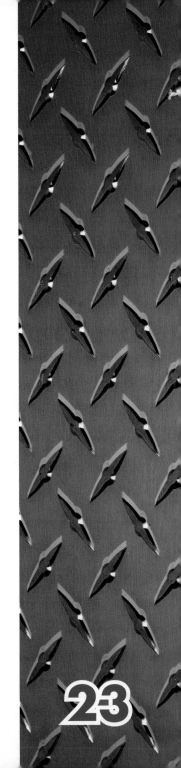

 Books

Bingham, Caroline. *DK Big Book of Airplanes.* New York: Dorling Kindersley, 2001.

Evans, Frank, and George Guzzi (illustrator). *All Aboard Airplanes.* New York: Grosset & Dunlap, 1994.

Pallotta, Jerry, Fred Stillwell, and Rob Bolster. *The Airplane Alphabet Book.* Watertown, MA: Charlesbridge Publishing, 1997.

 Web Sites

Visit our Web site for lots of links about airplanes:
http://www.childsworld.com/links
Note to parents, teachers, and librarians: We routinely check our Web links to make sure they're safe, active sites—so encourage your readers to check them out!

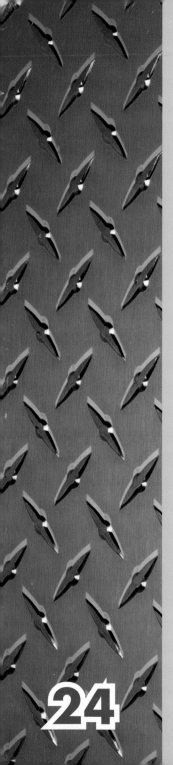

 # Index

 # About the Author

Even as a child, Cynthia Roberts knew she wanted to be a writer. She is always working to involve kids in reading and writing, and she loves spending time in the children's section of the library or bookstore. Cynthia enjoys gardening, traveling, and having fun with friends and family.